GW01374654

Gill Books
Hume Avenue
Park West
Dublin 12
www.gillbooks.ie

Gill Books is an imprint of M.H. Gill and Co.
© Gill Books 2023

978 07171 9983 9

Designed by Grant Kempster for Cloud King Creative
Written by Emily Stead
Proofread by Natasha Mac a'Bháird
Printed and bound by Białostockie Zakłady Graficzne S.A, Poland

The paper used in this book comes from the wood pulp of sustainably managed forests.

All rights reserved.
No part of this publication may be copied, reproduced or transmitted in any form or by any means, without written permission of the publishers.

A CIP catalogue record for this book is available from the British Library.

5 4 3 2 1

The publisher has taken every reasonable step to ensure the accuracy of the facts contained herein at the time of going to press, but can take no responsibility for any incorrect information arising from changes that may take place after this point.

The statistics and records in the book are correct as of 18 August 2023.

GO ON, THE GIRLS IN GREEN!

THE RISE AND RISE OF IRELAND'S WOMEN'S NATIONAL SOCCER TEAM

GILL BOOKS

CONTENTS

Introduction	8
Rising Up	10
Making History	12
Home Sweet Home	16
Number Crunching	18
Great Green: Áine O'Gorman	20
Courtney Brosnan	22
Grace Moloney	23
Megan Walsh	24
Izzy Atkinson	25
Diane Caldwell	26
Niamh Fahey	27
Aoife Mannion	28
Chloe Mustaki	29
Claire O'Riordan	30
Harriet Scott	31
Great Green: Louise Quinn	32
Lily Agg	34
Megan Connolly	35
Niamh Farrelly	36
Sinead Farrelly	37
Jamie Finn	38

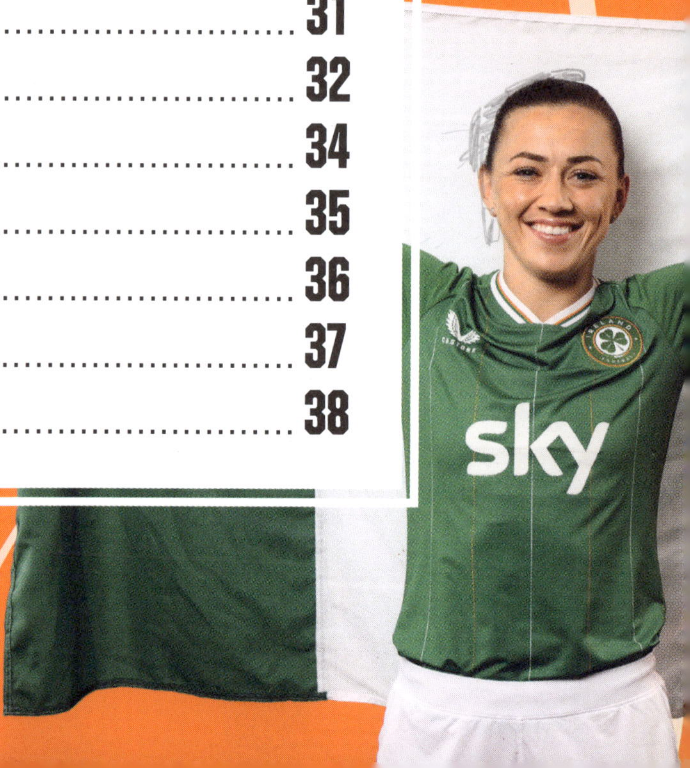

Ciara Grant	39
Ruesha Littlejohn	40
Roma McLaughlin	41
Lucy Quinn	42
Jess Ziu	43
Great Green: Katie McCabe	44
Amber Barrett	46
Kyra Carusa	47
Leanne Kiernan	48
Abbie Larkin	49
Heather Payne	50
Marissa Sheva	51
Great Green: Denise O'Sullivan	52
The Coach	54
The Future is Green!	56
Hall of Fame	58
Girls in Green: Down Under	60
Next Steps	64
Go for Glory!	66
Growing the Game	68
Answers	69

INTRODUCTION

Welcome to your **ultimate guide** to the **Ireland Women's National Team**, a celebration of **fifty years of football** since the team first kicked off their official game.

Join the **Girls in Green** on an **incredible journey** to their very first major tournament – the **Women's World Cup** in 2023 – and beyond!

Meet the **talented players in Ireland's squad** who have helped the team rise to their **highest-ever FIFA ranking**, learn about **past legends** and read our tips for **future stars**.

COME ON, YOU GIRLS IN GREEN!

#COYGIG   #OUTBELIEVE   #IRLWNT

RISING UP

Football in Ireland has been played by women from as early as the 1920s. Over the decades, the sport's popularity came in waves, with each generation of players fighting to be given the same opportunities as men to play the game they loved. Today, more women and girls are discovering the beautiful game than ever before, as players and fans, thanks to the huge strides taken by the players that came before them. Read on to learn about the history of women's football in Ireland, and the incredible rise of the women's national side!

1920s: KICKING OFF

10 May, 1920: Dundalk Ladies take on Manchester Corinthians in an unofficial international for a Republic of Ireland women's team.
1921: Unlike in England, no official ban is placed on women's football in Ireland.
1921: A combined Irish-Northeast England team lose to the famous Dick, Kerr Ladies team at Windsor Park.
1925: Matches due to be played in Dublin between Irish and French sides are cancelled by the Free State Purity League, which has strong objections to women athletes.
1927: A Dublin Ladies XI host Scottish side Rutherglen at Shamrock Rovers' ground in Milltown, Dublin. The match is billed as 'Scotland vs Ireland'.

1970s: A DECADE OF FIRSTS

10 May, 1970: A game advertised as a 'Ladies International Football Match' is played, with Dundalk Ladies or 'Ireland' facing 'England' represented by Corinthian Nomads. The match is played in Wales, as the English FA had banned women from playing on the grounds of their member clubs.
1973: The Women's Football Association of Ireland is established.
13 May, 1973: Ireland's first official international match is played: a 2–3 friendly victory over Wales in Llanelli.
30 June, 1973: The team's first home game is completed, with Ireland securing a 4–1 win over Northern Ireland in Dublin.

STAR: PAULA GORHAM

1930s-1950s: DECLINING FORTUNES

1930s: Women's football is in decline in Ireland, as a woman's place is deemed to be 'in the home'. While no women's teams compete in the Free State, many teams remain active in Northern Ireland.

1960s: INTEREST REVIVED

Indoor soccer leagues for both men and women see a surge in popularity of women's football.
1968: Dundalk Ladies are established and become Irish champions at club level, attracting crowds of thousands.
1969: Dundalk become founder members of the English Women's Football Association. Travelling to play in England comes at a cost, though, and trips are paid for through fundraising.

1980s: SLOW PROGRESS

Ireland enter teams, but fail to qualify for the Women's Euros in **1984**, **1987** and **1989**. Qualifiers are played against neighbours Northern Ireland, England and Scotland, with friendlies arranged against some of Europe's top sides.

STAR: LINDA GORMAN

2000s & 2010s: FALLING SHORT

2000: Ireland win the Celt Cup, a four-team tournament.
A lack of investment in the women's and girls' youth teams sees Ireland fall behind other European nations.
July 2003: FIFA place Ireland 38th in their official world rankings, the team's lowest-ever position.
April 2017: Players threaten to go on strike and see better pay and working conditions introduced for the current team and future generations.
Ireland fall short of qualification for all editions of the Women's Euros and Women's World Cup in these decades.

STAR: OLIVIA O'TOOLE

1990s: POOR RESULTS

November 1991: The first official Women's World Cup takes place in China. Twelve national teams take part, five of them from Europe. Ireland do not qualify.
20 September, 1992: Ireland suffer a 10–0 loss to Sweden in a Euro qualifier. The result remains the biggest defeat in the team's history.
1995: The FAI do not enter a team to try to qualify for the World Cup or Women's Euro.

STAR: EMMA BYRNE

2020s: REACHING RECORD HEIGHTS!

30 August, 2021: Equal pay for the men's and women's national teams is agreed, with the same match fees paid to the Boys and Girls in Green, in a momentous deal for Irish sport.
30 November, 2021: Ireland's women record their biggest-ever win. The World Cup qualifier at Tallaght Stadium ends Republic of Ireland 11–0 Georgia. Ireland narrowly miss out on reaching the play-offs for the Women's Euro 2022, finishing third behind Germany and Ukraine in a tough group.
11 October, 2022: Ireland qualify for the Women's World Cup 2023 for the first time in their history via a play-off against Scotland.
The Girls in Green lose just once in 10 games in 2022.
24 March, 2023: Ireland receive their highest ever FIFA Women's World Ranking – 22nd place.
Summer 2023: Ireland make their debut at the Women's World Cup in Australia and New Zealand. They are narrowly beaten by Australia and Canada and hold Nigeria to a draw.
Autumn 2023: The Girls in Green take on Northern Ireland, Hungary and Albania in League B of the new 2023/24 Women's Nations League.

STARS: KATIE MCCABE, ÁINE O'GORMAN, DENISE O'SULLIVAN

Amber Barrett scores the goal that seals Ireland's World Cup place.

MAKING HISTORY

Over nine exciting games in 2021 and 2022, the Girls in Green played with skill, grit and heart to do what no Irish women's national team had ever done before them – qualify for a major tournament! From treating the fans to a record goal-fest at Tallaght Stadium to their draw against the Olympic silver medallists to a historic play-off victory, here's how the Girls made it all the way to the Women's World Cup 2023 in Australia and New Zealand . . .

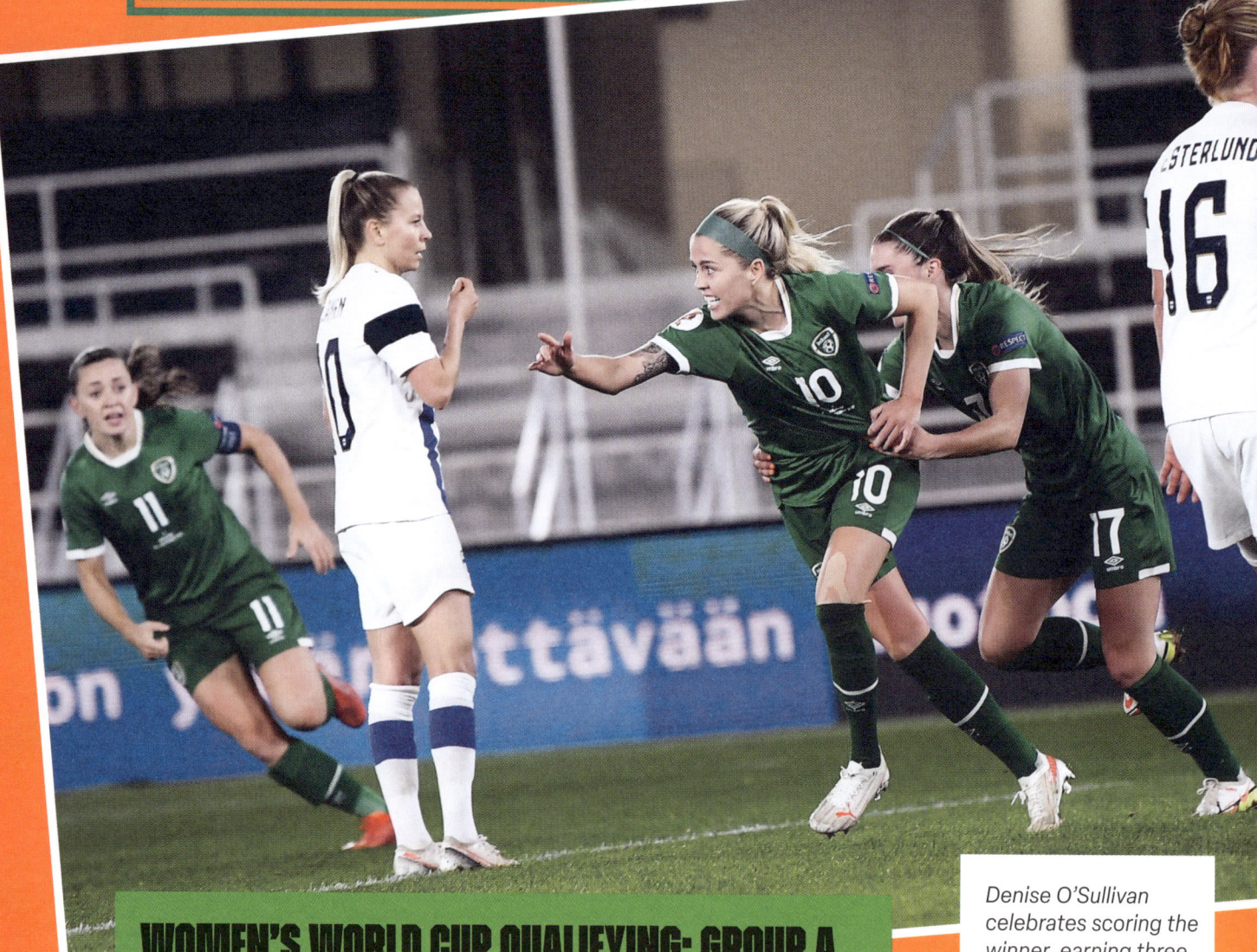

Denise O'Sullivan celebrates scoring the winner, earning three important points away to Finland.

WOMEN'S WORLD CUP QUALIFYING: GROUP A

Pos.	Team	Pld	W	D	L	GF	GA	GD	Pts
1	Sweden	8	7	1	0	32	2	30	22
2	**Rep. Ireland**	**8**	**5**	**2**	**1**	**26**	**4**	**22**	**17**
3	Finland	8	3	1	4	14	12	2	10
4	Slovakia	8	2	2	4	9	9	0	8
5	Georgia	8	0	0	8	0	54	-54	0

WORLD CUP QUALIFYING RESULTS

2021

Date				
21 Oct	Rep. Ireland	0–1	Sweden	
26 Oct	Finland	1–2	Rep. Ireland	
25 Nov	Rep. Ireland	1–1	Slovakia	
30 Nov	Rep. Ireland	11–0	Georgia	

Ireland scorers:

Connolly, O'Sullivan

McCabe

Bebia (og), Carusa, Lucy Quinn, O'Sullivan (3), McCabe (2), Noonan, Barrett, Connolly

Megan Connolly adds an incredible eleventh goal in Ireland's record win over Georgia at Tallaght Stadium.

Skipper Katie McCabe scores the equaliser against Olympic silver medallists Sweden in Gothenburg.

Lily Agg blasts her header past the Finland keeper to secure Ireland's place in the World Cup play-offs.

WORLD CUP QUALIFYING RESULTS

2022				IWNT scorers:
12 Apr	Sweden	1–1	Rep. Ireland	McCabe
27 Jun	Georgia	0–9	Rep. Ireland	McCabe (3), Fahey, Connolly, Louise Quinn (2), Larkin, O'Sullivan
1 Sept	Rep. Ireland	1–0	Finland	Agg
6 Sept	Slovakia	0–1	Rep. Ireland	O'Sullivan
11 Oct	Scotland	0–1	Rep. Ireland	Barrett

A NIGHT NEVER TO BE FORGOTTEN!

Hampden Park in Glasgow was the destination for the **biggest match in the team's history** in October 2022. With experience of playing at a World Cup and Women's Euros, home side Scotland went into the match as favourites. **Courtney Brosnan saved a penalty** before super sub **Amber Barrett fired home** with her first touches of the ball in the second half. The Girls in Green hung on to book their place at the **World Cup in 2023**!

Katie McCabe led by example in a strong team performance at Hampden.

SCOTLAND 0 — **REPUBLIC OF IRELAND** 1

1 Courtney BROSNAN
2 Jamie FINN
5 Niamh FAHEY
4 Louise QUINN
7 Diane CALDWELL
6 Megan CAMPBELL
13 Áine O'GORMAN
12 Lily AGG
10 Denise O'SULLIVAN
11 Katie McCABE (captain)
14 Heather PAYNE

SUB:
9 Amber BARRETT

HOME SWEET HOME

Tallaght Stadium in South Dublin is where Ireland's Women's National Team play most of their home matches, with crowds growing every year. While Tallaght may be tiny compared to the Aviva Stadium or Croke Park – where 10 times the amount of fans can cram in – the atmosphere at the stadium is always incredible.

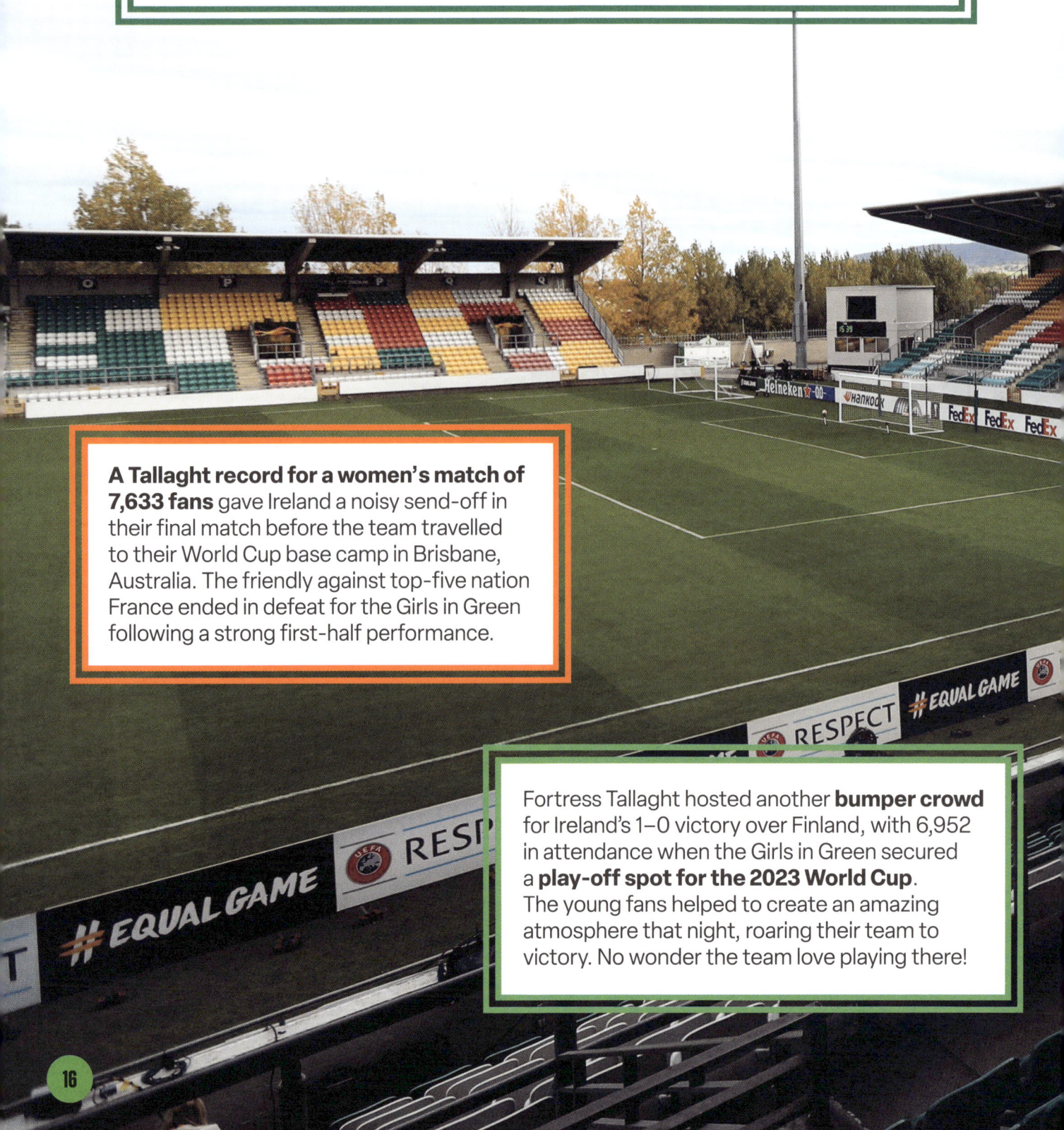

A Tallaght record for a women's match of 7,633 fans gave Ireland a noisy send-off in their final match before the team travelled to their World Cup base camp in Brisbane, Australia. The friendly against top-five nation France ended in defeat for the Girls in Green following a strong first-half performance.

Fortress Tallaght hosted another **bumper crowd** for Ireland's 1–0 victory over Finland, with 6,952 in attendance when the Girls in Green secured a **play-off spot for the 2023 World Cup**. The young fans helped to create an amazing atmosphere that night, roaring their team to victory. No wonder the team love playing there!

FACT FILE:
NAME: Tallaght Stadium
LOCATION: Tallaght, South Dublin
CAPACITY: 8,000
OPENED: 13 March, 2009
HOME TO: Shamrock Rovers FC

Tallaght Stadium played host to the Girls' biggest ever win in November 2021 – an 11–0 victory over Georgia!

Lily Agg's second-half goal proved the winner against Finland and sent the Tallaght crowd wild!

NOW TURN THE PAGE TO GET TO KNOW IRELAND'S FAMOUS GIRLS IN GREEN.

NUMBER CRUNCHING

Whether you're a Girls in Green superfan or just joining the team on their incredible journey, here are the all-important numbers about the WNT you need to know to impress your family and fellow fans.

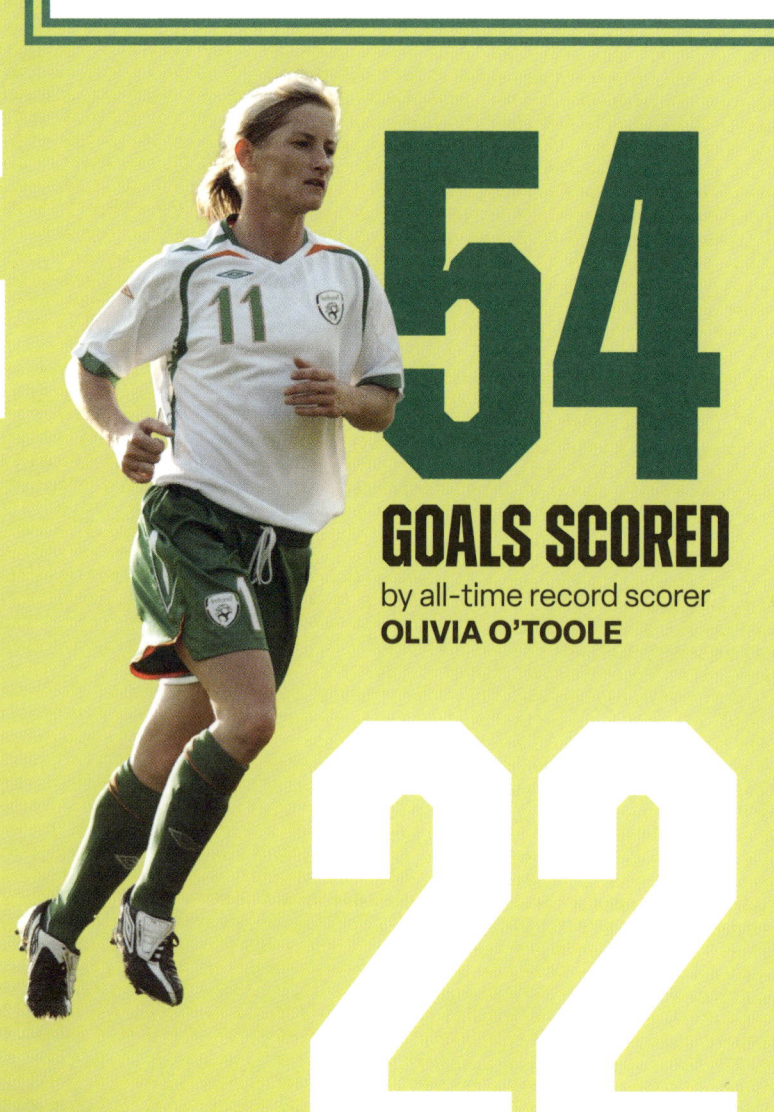

134
MOST CAPS
Goalkeeping great **EMMA BYRNE**

54
GOALS SCORED
by all-time record scorer **OLIVIA O'TOOLE**

11-0
RECORD SCORE
v **GEORGIA**
30 November, 2021

1
WOMEN'S WORLD CUP APPEARANCE 2023

22
HIGHEST-EVER FIFA WOMEN'S WORLD RANKING 24 March, 2023

18

2-3
WALES v REPUBLIC OF IRELAND
The result of the **FIRST OFFICIAL INTERNATIONAL MATCH** 13 May, 1973

11
The shirt number of Captain Fantastic **KATIE McCABE**

23
Heroic Girls in Green made up the **WORLD CUP SQUAD**

2021
The FAI announces an **EQUAL PAY** deal for its men's and women's teams

75,784
A **RECORD ATTENDANCE** for an IWNT match: Australia v Ireland, Stadium Australia, 20 July 2023

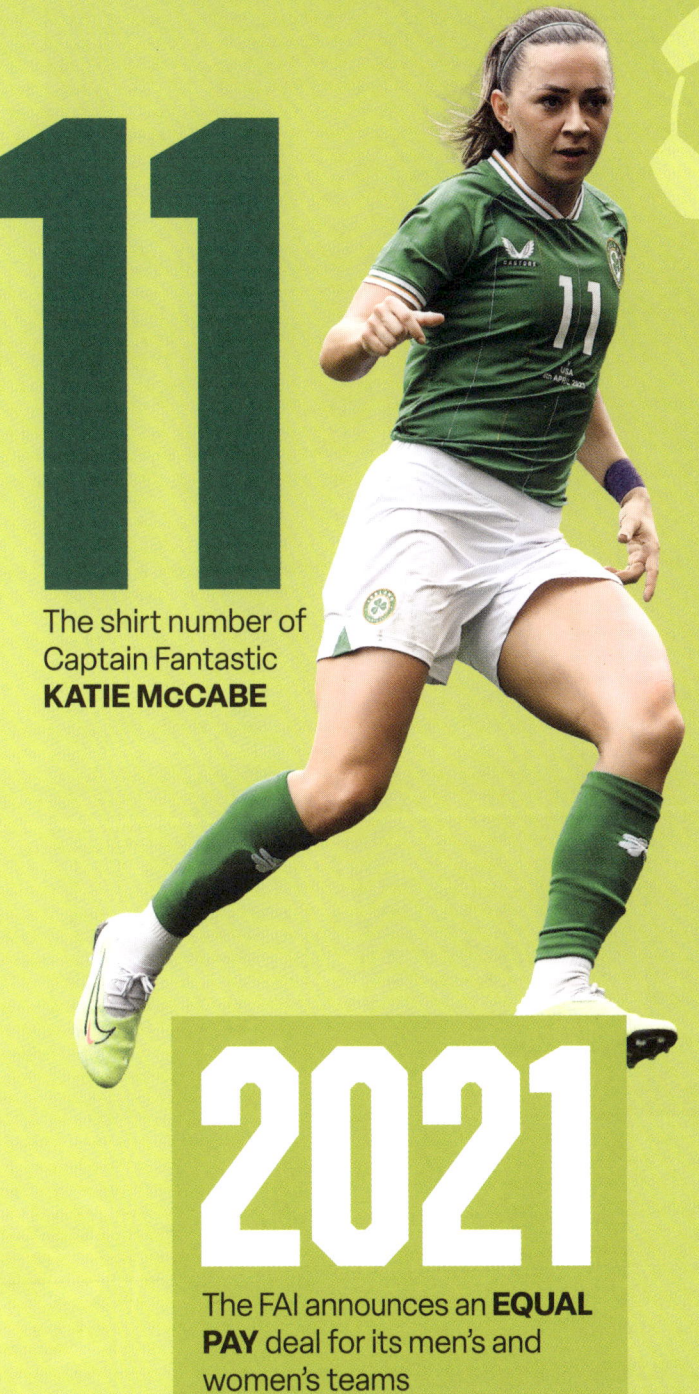

1 GOAL SCORED
at the 2023 Women's World Cup. A set-piece stunner from **KATIE McCABE**

GREAT GREEN

ÁINE O'GORMAN

POSITION: Forward / defender
IRELAND CAPS: 120+
IRELAND GOALS: 10+
DATE OF BIRTH: 13 May, 1989
PLACE OF BIRTH: Wicklow (Co. Wicklow)
CURRENT CLUB: Shamrock Rovers (Ireland)
HEIGHT: 1 m 64 cm
FAVOURED FOOT: Right

PROFILE:

An **inspiration to all young Irish players**, Áine O'Gorman is proof that you can still play at a high level on home soil, having spent most of her career playing for Dublin clubs in the Irish top flight. The **most-capped Girl in Green** in the current squad, she's won **more than 120 caps** since breaking into the senior team at the age of 16 with a debut against Denmark. Áine is a **natural goalscorer** who has mostly played as a deadly striker or winger, but has also filled in as a full-back when called upon by Vera Pauw. She retired from international football in 2018, but returned in 2020 and **helped to make history** as part of the Ireland squad that reached their first World Cup in 2023.

FOOTBALL JOURNEY:

Enniskerry FC was where **talented sports star** Áine began her football journey, playing alongside boys, after begging her big brother to take her along to training. If the team was missing a player, six-year-old Áine would step in to play. She then represented Stella Maris football club, and later starred for Bray Emmets playing Gaelic football, although **football remained her first love**.

Watching her hero Olivia O'Toole play at Richmond Park growing up inspired Áine to follow her dream of playing for Ireland, and she didn't have too long to wait, claiming a spot in the **senior squad from the age of 16**. Her first appearance was in the Algarve Cup in 2006, while the Wicklow-born player also featured for Ireland's Under-17s and Under-19s.

Seventeen years later, Áine still feels the same **buzz of excitement** pulling on a green jersey as she did on her debut, but the experienced forward is the first to admit that representing the national side hasn't always been easy. Playing in a World Cup tournament at times looked a distant dream for Áine, who remembers the team having to threaten to strike in 2017. Only a few years ago, the players were still forced to get changed in public toilets on the way to matches and had to share tracksuits with younger squads. Áine put her international career on hold in 2018, returning to **use her voice in helping to win equal pay** and better opportunities for the Girls in Green in 2021.

Some memorable moments with the squad include when **Áine captained Ireland for the first time** in 2015 against world champions,

Áine had more caps than any other player in Ireland's World Cup squad.

United States, while the following year she **netted a hat-trick** in a 9-0 win over Montenegro – a record-equalling score that stood until 2021. In 2022, Áine was the **only home-based player** in Ireland's famous play-off victory over Scotland, a surprise inclusion on the right wing in Vera Pauw's starting eleven.

A couple of seasons with Doncaster Rovers Belles in the English league apart, Áine has chosen to play her club football at home in Ireland, as an amateur. She has been the Women's National League Top Goalscorer an **incredible five times** while on the books at Peamount United, earning a host of trophies along the way. In 2023, rival club Shamrock Rovers won Áine's signature on their return to the WNL. When not on the pitch, Áine has been kept busy working as a personal trainer, a TV and radio pundit and has already completed some of her coaching badges. She also became a mum to baby James in 2022.

WORLD CUP STAR ★
COURTNEY BROSNAN

POSITION: Goalkeeper
IRELAND CAPS: 20+
IRELAND CLEAN SHEETS: 10+
DATE OF BIRTH: 10 November, 1995
PLACE OF BIRTH: New Jersey (USA)
CURRENT CLUB: Everton (England)

PROFILE:
Born and raised in New Jersey, USA, keeper Courtney moved to play soccer in Europe as soon as her college days were over – first in France, then in England's Women's Super League with West Ham United and Everton. Having chosen to represent Ireland, Courtney made her international debut against Germany in 2020. She has since established herself as **Ireland's Number 1** between the sticks and is known for her mental strength and **super shot-stopping**. Her crucial penalty save against Scotland helped Ireland qualify for the World Cup, while she kept a clean sheet against Nigeria at the tournament.

GRACE MOLONEY

WORLD CUP STAR

POSITION: Goalkeeper
IRELAND CAPS: 5+
IRELAND CLEAN SHEETS: 1+
DATE OF BIRTH: 1 March, 1993
PLACE OF BIRTH: Slough (England)
CURRENT CLUB: Reading (England)

PROFILE:
Although she was born and raised in England, Grace **dreamed of playing for Ireland** from a young age. It was a dream that came true when the young goalkeeper was called up to the national squad aged just 15. She describes her first competitive start against Germany in 2020 as the 'best day of [her] life', while her hero growing up was legendary goalkeeper Emma Byrne. Grace has spent the whole of her senior career on the books at local club Reading, where her **shot-stopping** and **distribution** are two of her key strengths.

WORLD CUP STAR

MEGAN WALSH

POSITION: Goalkeeper
IRELAND CAPS: 1+
IRELAND CLEAN SHEETS: 0
DATE OF BIRTH: 12 November, 1994
PLACE OF BIRTH: Bromsgrove (England)
PREVIOUS CLUB: Brighton & Hove Albion (England)

PROFILE:

Another English-born keeper, Megan represented the Lionesses at youth levels but was keen to join the **Girls in Green** when she learned she qualified through her Wexford-born grandfather. In November 2021, Megan joined Vera Pauw's squad for the first time, but with Courtney Brosnan established as Ireland's first-choice stopper, caps have been hard to come by. Megan's **solo cap** so far came against Russia in the Pinatar Cup in 2022, where she impressed Vera Pauw with some **stunning saves**. Megan was with Brighton & Hove Albion until the summer of 2023.

IZZY ATKINSON

WORLD CUP STAR ★

POSITION: Defender
IRELAND CAPS: 5+
IRELAND GOALS: 0
DATE OF BIRTH: 17 July, 2001
PLACE OF BIRTH: Rush (Co. Dublin)
CURRENT CLUB: West Ham United (England)

PROFILE:

A **last-minute addition** to Vera Pauw's World Cup squad, Izzy was thrilled to earn a spot to travel Down Under with the Girls in Green and make two appearances from the bench. The player who began her senior career with Shelbourne shows her best form out **wide on the left,** whether operating as a wing-back or further up the field. She made her senior international debut in January 2018, away to Portugal, as a **16-year-old**, while her first start came against Belgium the following year. Izzy joined WSL side West Ham United from Celtic ahead of the 2022/23 season.

WORLD CUP STAR ★

DIANE CALDWELL

POSITION: Defender
IRELAND CAPS: 95+
IRELAND GOALS: 1+
DATE OF BIRTH: 11 September, 1988
PLACE OF BIRTH: Balbriggan (Co. Dublin)
CURRENT CLUB: Reading (England)

PROFILE:

One of the **most experienced Girls in Green**, Diane is a top central defender who began her career with Raheny United before moving to the United States to play college soccer. She has since played for clubs in the USA, Iceland, Germany and England. After first representing Ireland's Under-17s at the age of just 14, Diane progressed through the ranks to make her **senior debut aged 17**. The defender scored her debut international goal against Northern Ireland at the 2013 Cyprus Cup, and captained Ireland to third place at the 2022 Pinatar Cup in Spain.

NIAMH FAHEY

WORLD CUP STAR ★

POSITION: Defender
IRELAND CAPS: 110+
IRELAND GOALS: 1+
DATE OF BIRTH: 13 October, 1987
PLACE OF BIRTH: Galway (Co. Galway)
CURRENT CLUB: Liverpool (England)

PROFILE:
Comfortable playing in central defence or as a defensive midfielder, Niamh started out in soccer with her hometown club, Salthill Devon. She also won national trophies playing Gaelic football growing up. At club level, Niamh is one of the **game's most decorated players**, having won a host of trophies with WSL sides Arsenal and Chelsea. A lifelong Liverpool fan, she joined the Reds in 2018, and now captains the side. Her Ireland debut came against Portugal in 2007, while the **three-time winner** of the **FAI Women's Senior Player of the Year** award now has more than 100 international caps. Niamh played in all three Group games at the World Cup.

SQUAD STAR ★ AOIFE MANNION

POSITION: Defender
IRELAND CAPS: 1+
IRELAND GOALS: 0
DATE OF BIRTH: 24 September, 1995
PLACE OF BIRTH: Solihull (England)
CURRENT CLUB: Manchester United (England)

PROFILE:
An **experienced defender** in the Women's Super League, Aoife can play anywhere across the defensive backline. She grew up playing for England's underage sides before **switching to become a senior with Ireland** to the delight of her Mayo-born father. Playing mixed Gaelic football until the age of 14 helped to toughen her up, while England winger Jack Grealish was once an opponent. Her debut for the Girls in Green came in February 2023, against China PR, while her recovery from a knee injury came just too late to make the final World Cup squad.

CHLOE MUSTAKI

WORLD CUP STAR

POSITION: Defender
IRELAND CAPS: 5+
IRELAND GOALS: 0
DATE OF BIRTH: 29 July, 1995
PLACE OF BIRTH: Ohio (United States)
CURRENT CLUB: Bristol City (England)

PROFILE:

Globe-trotting Chloe was born in the United States, but was raised in Paris and Dublin. It was on the streets of Cabinteely that Chloe first discovered her **love of soccer**, where she teamed up with friends and her brother. At 16, Chloe signed for Peamount United, **winning the league title** in her first season with the club. The teenager later overcame cancer and a serious ACL knee injury before making a belated **international debut** for the Girls in Green against Russia in 2022 at the Pinatar Cup. She recently helped Bristol City secure promotion to the English WSL as champions.

WORLD CUP STAR

CLAIRE O'RIORDAN

POSITION: Defender
IRELAND CAPS: 15+
IRELAND GOALS: 1+
DATE OF BIRTH: 12 October, 1994
PLACE OF BIRTH: Newcastle West (Co. Limerick)
CURRENT CLUB: Standard Liège (Belgium)

PROFILE:
Born in Limerick, Claire first caught the attention of soccer scouts while playing in the Women's National League with Wexford Youths as a **Number 9**. Unlike many of her teammates, Claire didn't feature for Ireland's youth sides, instead it was only when she began playing in the German women's Bundesliga that her talents were truly recognised – after she **switched positions to become a centre-back**. Her debut for Ireland came at the 2016 Cyprus Women's Cup, against Hungary, while Claire grabbed her first international goal against Zambia in June 2023. She joined Belgian side Standard Liège just before the World Cup.

HARRIET SCOTT

SQUAD STAR ★

POSITION: Defender
IRELAND CAPS: 20+
IRELAND GOALS: 0
DATE OF BIRTH: 10 February, 1993
PLACE OF BIRTH: Reading (England)
PREVIOUS CLUB: Birmingham City (England)

PROFILE:

A **battling left-back**, Harriet was part of Ireland's squad that finished as runners-up in the 2010 Women's Under-17 Championship, and made the quarter-finals of the Under-17 World Cup that same year. She burst on to the international scene with the senior side with some **solid defensive performances** that saw her named Ireland's Senior Women's Player of the Year in 2017. In club football, the defender began her career in the WSL with Reading, before a move to Birmingham City in 2018. Following the World Cup, Harriet decided to step away from football and work as a doctor, after completing her studies in medicine.

GREAT GREEN

LOUISE QUINN

POSITION: Defender
IRELAND CAPS: 105+
IRELAND GOALS: 15+
DATE OF BIRTH: 17 June, 1990
PLACE OF BIRTH: Blessington (Co. Wicklow)
CURRENT CLUB: Birmingham City (England)
HEIGHT: 1 m 83 cm
FAVOURED FOOT: Right

PROFILE:

Towering defender Louise is one of the **squad's most experienced players**, with her 100th cap earned in 2022 – she made sure her name was on the scoresheet that game too! Her **quality in the centre of defence** has seen Louise ply her skills in some of Europe's top leagues, starring for famous clubs in Sweden, Italy and England. She has twice been named the **FAI Senior Women's Player of the Year**, in 2013 and 2019, since first making her international debut as a fresh-faced 17-year-old while on the books at Peamount United. A **true leader**, Louise was once hailed as a 'tiger' by Vera Pauw, for the strength and fight she brings to the Irish national side!

FOOTBALL JOURNEY:

Blessington Boys Under-6s was the club where Louise was introduced to the beautiful game, before joining her first girls' team, Lakeside of Wicklow, in her teens. Growing up, she was also a talented Gaelic player, where she went in goal for Blessington's adult team from a very young age. Louise's next step in football was to Peamount United, aged 14, while she was given the captain's armband by the age of 16. In 2011, she skippered the Peas to the last **32 of the Champions League**.

Her international career began early too, with Louise receiving a call-up to Ireland's Under-17s while still only 14. She was later chosen to captain the Under-19s, and made her debut for the senior side aged 20 against Poland.

After her successes with Peamount, Louise began to believe she could make it as a professional, and considered offers from clubs overseas. The dependable defender spent three years with Eskilstuna United in Sweden, where she grew into one of the **best defenders in the league**.

A move to the UK came next, in 2017, but her new club, Notts County, ran into money troubles and folded. Instead, Louise followed in the footsteps of **Emma Byrne** and **Katie McCabe** and moved to North London with **champions Arsenal**, where she won the WSL Cup, and the league title in 2018–19, ever-present at the heart of the Gunners' defence.

In November 2022, 14 years after making her debut, Vera Pauw presented Louise with a **golden cap** to celebrate the defender's **100th appearance** before the friendly against Morocco. Louise scored the third goal in a 4–0 win. An excellent header of the ball, the **Mighty Quinn** has also chipped in with 15 goals and counting for her country – not bad for a defender! One of her favourite matches in a green jersey was the play-off victory over Scotland that sealed Ireland's place at the World Cup in Australia and New Zealand, which showed young fans that dreams can come true.

When not on Ireland duty, Louise plays for **Birmingham City** in the Women's Championship, having spent a season at Fiorentina in Italy's top league. The **Blues' captain**, Louise loves playing alongside a number of Ireland teammates at the club. She remains a fine deputy to skipper Katie McCabe with the national side too, as they strive to help the **Girls in Green reach new heights**.

Louise celebrates scoring at Tallaght with teammate Stephanie Roche (Zambra).

WORLD CUP STAR ★ LILY AGG

POSITION: Midfielder
IRELAND CAPS: 25+
IRELAND GOALS: 1+
DATE OF BIRTH: 17 December, 1993
PLACE OF BIRTH: Brighton (England)
PREVIOUS CLUB: London City Lionesses (England)

PROFILE:
Lily grew up on the south coast of England and represented the Young Lionesses up to Under-19 level. But when Vera Pauw reached out to the midfielder to become a **Girl in Green**, Lily applied for her Irish citizenship. **Scoring on her debut** against the Philippines was her reward, while her next strike was the **crucial goal** that secured Ireland's play-off spot and ultimately qualification for the World Cup. Lily featured against both Canada and Nigeria Down Under. The midfielder has played for **eight different clubs** so far, and would love to be a soccer coach when her playing days are over.

MEGAN CONNOLLY

WORLD CUP STAR

POSITION: Midfielder
IRELAND CAPS: 40+
IRELAND GOALS: 1+
DATE OF BIRTH: 7 March, 1997
PLACE OF BIRTH: Cork (Co. Cork)
PREVIOUS CLUB: Brighton & Hove Albion (England)

PROFILE:

A soccer star from the age of six, Megan blossomed into a **fine midfielder** who loves to get forward. From a sporting family, her brother plays Gaelic football, while her dad coached his daughter's teams growing up. Megan was regularly on the scoresheet with Ireland's youth teams and made her senior debut against the United States in 2016. Her first senior goal in a green shirt came against Montenegro back in 2016; since then, she has become one of the **squad's most experienced players**. Possessing **fantastic technique**, Megan is known for her **set-piece delivery** for club and country. She played every minute of Ireland's World Cup campaign in Australia.

SQUAD STAR ★ NIAMH FARRELLY

POSITION: Defender / Midfielder
IRELAND CAPS: 1+
IRELAND GOALS: 0
DATE OF BIRTH: 15 April, 1999
PLACE OF BIRTH: Dublin (Co. Dublin)
CURRENT CLUB: Parma (Italy)

PROFILE:

Able to operate centrally in defence or midfield, Niamh has **represented Ireland at every underage level**, captaining Ireland's Under-19s. The former Peamount United youngster signed her first professional contract with Glasgow City in 2021 before seeking a new challenge at current club Parma, who play in Italy's top women's league. She won her first senior international cap in January 2019 against Belgium while still a teenager, and was **part of the victorious squad** that beat Scotland to reach the 2023 Women's World Cup. While injury limited Niamh's minutes for the Girls in Green in recent months, she believes she's now back on her **best form**.

SINEAD FARRELLY

WORLD CUP STAR

POSITION: Midfielder
IRELAND CAPS: 1+
IRELAND GOALS: 0
DATE OF BIRTH: 16 November, 1989
PLACE OF BIRTH: Havertown (USA)
CURRENT CLUB: NJ/NY Gotham (USA)

PROFILE:
Another player with US roots, Sinead spent part of her childhood in Ireland as her father hails from Cavan. She represented the United States from Under-15 to Under-23 levels, mostly while playing in America's NWSL. Sinead made an **incredible return** to the game after retiring for more than six seasons following a car crash, and made a **late switch of international teams**, winning her first cap for the IWNT at the age of 33. The midfielder played all three Group matches at the World Cup – with a broken arm!

SQUAD STAR ★ JAMIE FINN

POSITION: Defender / Midfielder
IRELAND CAPS: 15+
IRELAND GOALS: 0
DATE OF BIRTH: 21 April, 1998
PLACE OF BIRTH: Dublin (Co. Dublin)
CURRENT CLUB: Birmingham City (England)

PROFILE:
Swords native Jamie started her soccer career at the age of five with mixed side Swords Manor. As a schoolgirl, she **captained both Ireland's Under-17 and Under-19 sides**. Strong in defence or midfield, Jamie was first called into the senior squad following some **fine performances** for club side Shelbourne. She made her first start against Greece in November 2019, playing in a defensive midfield role. Before she became a full-time soccer player with English side Birmingham City, Jamie worked as a personal trainer. While she's a **regular starter** for the Blues, Jamie's next goal is to win more caps in a green shirt too.

CIARA GRANT

WORLD CUP STAR ★

POSITION: Midfielder
IRELAND CAPS: 15+
IRELAND GOALS: 0
DATE OF BIRTH: 11 June, 1993
PLACE OF BIRTH: Letterkenny (Co. Donegal)
CURRENT CLUB: Heart of Midlothian (Scotland)

PROFILE:
Donegal midfielder Ciara earned her first cap for the national side back in 2012, after she **captained the squad that finished as runners-up** in the 2010 Women's Under-17 Championship. She stepped away from soccer while studying and working as a doctor, but couldn't resist the call of the green shirt for too long. Ciara's **return to form** in the 2020/21 season saw Vera Pauw recall her to the senior squad for the record win over Georgia. The midfielder signed her first professional contract in 2022 with Glasgow side Rangers, helping the club to win their first Scottish Premiership title in an **unbeaten season**.

WORLD CUP STAR

RUESHA LITTLEJOHN

POSITION: Midfielder
IRELAND CAPS: 75+
IRELAND GOALS: 5+
DATE OF BIRTH: 3 July, 1990
PLACE OF BIRTH: Glasgow, Scotland
PREVIOUS CLUB: Aston Villa (England)

PROFILE:

Glaswegian Ruesha hasn't looked back since swapping her navy blue shirt for the **emerald green of Ireland**, having played for Scotland as a schoolgirl. Since making her debut back in 2012 against Hungary, Ruesha has now reached **75 caps** for Ireland. Playing as an attacking midfielder she is **brilliant at breaking up the play** and starting attacking moves, while she's a **strong finisher** in front of goal too. Ruesha made the **first eleven** for all three of the team's World Cup matches. A busy career at club level has seen her represent more than 10 different clubs in Scotland, England and Sweden.

ROMA MCLAUGHLIN

SQUAD STAR ★

POSITION: Midfielder
IRELAND CAPS: 10+
IRELAND GOALS: 0
DATE OF BIRTH: 6 March, 1998
PLACE OF BIRTH: Greencastle (Co. Donegal)
CURRENT CLUB: Fortuna Hjørring (Denmark)

PROFILE:

Hotly tipped as a teenager playing for Peamount United and Shelbourne, Roma made her Ireland debut in 2016. Four years of playing **college football in the USA**, starring for Central Connecticut State University, followed, but Roma found caps for the national side hard to come by. Vera Pauw recalled the **hard-working midfielder** to the squad in the summer of 2021, impressed by Roma's fine form Stateside. She signed for Danish club Fortuna Hjørring in January 2023 on a full-time contract, and is now into **double figures** for international appearances.

WORLD CUP STAR ★

LUCY QUINN

POSITION: Midfielder / Forward
IRELAND CAPS: 10+
IRELAND GOALS: 1+
DATE OF BIRTH: 29 September, 1993
PLACE OF BIRTH: Southampton (England)
CURRENT CLUB: Birmingham City (England)

PROFILE:

Having secured her Irish passport in 2021, Lucy made her debut in Ireland's victory over Australia that September, with her free kick helping her side earn a memorable win. Since then, the roving midfielder has earned more than a dozen international caps, while **adding firepower to Ireland's attack** with her ability to score quality goals. Her official debut strike came in the Girls in Green's record win over Georgia at Tallaght Stadium. Lucy signed her first professional contract with Birmingham City in 2017 and re-signed for a second spell there in 2021. She made two World Cup appearances, including one start.

JESS ZIU

SQUAD STAR ★

POSITION: Midfielder
IRELAND CAPS: 10+
IRELAND GOALS: 0
DATE OF BIRTH: 6 June, 2002
PLACE OF BIRTH: Dublin (Co. Dublin)
CURRENT CLUB: West Ham United (England)

PROFILE:

Jess's mother was originally against the idea of her daughter playing football, but finally bought Jess a pair of boots when her **talent became too good to ignore**. Her rapid rise at Shelbourne caught the attention of the national side – Jess had just turned 16 when she made her senior debut in the 4-0 win over Northern Ireland in August 2018. Jess can play as a wing-back or in midfield and possesses the **pace, skill and confidence** to carry the ball past opponents. Sadly, a bad knee injury saw her miss most of the 2022/23 season, ruling her out of the World Cup squad. But with youth on her side, Jess should earn a recall when fully fit.

GREAT GREEN
KATIE MCCABE

POSITION: Defender / Midfielder / Forward
IRELAND CAPS: 70+
IRELAND GOALS: 20+
DATE OF BIRTH: 21 September, 1995
PLACE OF BIRTH: Kilnamanagh (Co. Dublin)
CURRENT CLUB: Arsenal (England)
HEIGHT: 1 m 64 cm
FAVOURED FOOT: Left

PROFILE:
When it comes to Great Greens, they don't come much greater than Katie McCabe. Ireland's **left-footed captain** plays with her heart on her sleeve, whether as a full-back, midfielder or on the wing. Katie's senior debut came aged 19, while she became captain at just 21 – Ireland's **youngest-ever skipper** has worn the armband since 2017. Off the pitch, in 2021, Katie played a key role in persuading the FAI to give equal pay to their men's and women's teams for each match. She's played in the WSL with Arsenal since 2015, won four major trophies, seen Champions League action and captained the Gunners too. **World class!**

FOOTBALL JOURNEY:

A **kid from Kilnamanagh** who grew up in the shadows of Tallaght Stadium, Katie first kicked a ball around with her dad aged five or six. She was the only girl at her first junior club Kilnamanagh AFC and later Crumlin United, until she joined a girls' side, Templeogue United, at the age of 10. As one of 11 siblings, Katie has been a **team player from day one**, while the whole family loves sport. Her elder brother Gary was a winger for a number of League of Ireland clubs, while younger sister Lauryn has dreams of becoming a professional soccer star just like Katie – she currently plays for Ireland's youth sides.

Katie signed her first senior contract with Raheny United as soon as she turned 16, with the club thrilled to capture the signature of one of the **nation's brightest young talents**. There, she had to overcome a broken leg, and fought back to score **23 goals** in the 2014/15 season. Her opening goal in the FAI Women's Cup – a 35-yard screamer from a free kick – helped win the cup for Raheny and caught the attention of scouts from some of the UK's top clubs.

A **dream move to Arsenal at the age of 20** came just months after Katie made her international debut with the senior Girls in Green against Hungary at the Istria Cup. Her first season with the Gunners wasn't as easy as Katie had hoped, with some small injuries keeping her out of the side. So, keen to show why she deserved to be playing, Katie went on loan to Glasgow City. There, she began to show her **real quality on the ball**, as well as her fierce self-confidence. Ireland's next head coach Colin Bell was impressed enough to make **21-year-old Katie his captain**, when legendary goalkeeper and former Gunners teammate Emma Byrne retired.

On her return to Arsenal, Katie became an important player at the club, excelling anywhere on the left, from full-back to forward, creating amazing assists for her teammates and chipping in with some incredible goals herself. In the 2022/23 season she made 38 appearances and was voted the Gunners' Player of the Season.

Her **strong work ethic** also helped carry the Girls in Green to their historic first World Cup in Australia and New Zealand in 2023, where she delivered some **top-class performances on the world stage**. Who could forget her incredible 'Olimpico' goal against Canada? Now one of the squad's most experienced players, the super skipper's next goal is to lead the team to more major tournaments, while helping to push the game on for future generations.

Katie has been a leader on and off the pitch for the Girls in Green.

WORLD CUP STAR

AMBER BARRETT

POSITION: Forward
IRELAND CAPS: 35+
IRELAND GOALS: 5+
DATE OF BIRTH: 16 January, 1996
PLACE OF BIRTH: Milford (Co. Donegal)
CURRENT CLUB: Standard Liège (Belgium)

PROFILE:

The **former Peamount United hotshot** earned her first cap for the Girls in Green against Northern Ireland in September 2017 at the age of 21. Her **debut goal** came a year later against Slovakia. Amber will forever be remembered as the scorer of *that* goal – the one that earned **victory over Scotland** in the Qualifying Play-Off and sent Ireland to the 2023 Women's World Cup. Her goal celebration was dedicated to the 10 people who lost their lives in the Creeslough explosion tragedy that took place just days before the match. Amber featured once from the bench at the **World Cup**, against Canada, earning her 37th international cap.

46

KYRA CARUSA

WORLD CUP STAR ★

POSITION: Forward
IRELAND CAPS: 10+
IRELAND GOALS: 1+
DATE OF BIRTH: 14 November, 1995
PLACE OF BIRTH: San Diego (USA)
CURRENT CLUB: San Diego Wave (USA)

PROFILE:

Kyra is an **exciting striker** who loves **creating assists** as much as she does **getting on the scoresheet** herself. Her hold-up play and **strong mentality** are two of Kyra's special qualities in the Number 9 role. The US-born star made her Ireland debut in the Euro 2022 qualifier away to Montenegro, and has scored goals against Georgia and Morocco. Kyra led the line in **all three** of Ireland's games at the World Cup in Australia. In club football, she joined NWSL side San Diego Wave in August 2023, moving from London City Lionesses.

SQUAD STAR ★ LEANNE KIERNAN

POSITION: Forward
IRELAND CAPS: 25+
IRELAND GOALS: 1+
DATE OF BIRTH: 27 April, 1999
PLACE OF BIRTH: Bailieborough (Co. Cavan)
CURRENT CLUB: Liverpool (England)

PROFILE:

Leanne was first called up to the senior squad aged 17, and made her debut against Wales. A **talented Number 9**, she can also **operate on the wing** and has represented the young Girls in Green at Under-17 and Under-19 levels. Leanne began her career with Shelbourne, **winning three trophies**, before a move to Women's Super League club West Ham United while still a teenager. She switched sides to Liverpool next, scoring **13 goals** to help the club return to the WSL as champions. After sitting out most of the 2022/23 season and World Cup with an ankle injury, Leanne is keen to make up for lost time.

ABBIE LARKIN

WORLD CUP STAR ★

POSITION: Forward
IRELAND CAPS: 10+
IRELAND GOALS: 1+
DATE OF BIRTH: 27 April, 2005
PLACE OF BIRTH: Dublin (Co. Dublin)
CURRENT CLUB: Shamrock Rovers

PROFILE:

Teenager Abbie Larkin earned her first senior call-up for the Pinatar Cup squad in February 2022 aged 16, **impressing on her debut** against Russia. Her **debut goal** for the Girls in Green came in the 9–0 away victory over Georgia in June 2022, assisted by her then Shelbourne teammate Jess Ziu. Abbie is known for her leadership skills on and off the pitch, and has captained Ireland at Under-17 level. It was a girlhood dream realised to be **chosen for Ireland's World Cup squad**, while she was just 18 when she made her World Cup debut as a sub against Australia in front of more than 75,000 fans.

WORLD CUP STAR ★

HEATHER PAYNE

POSITION: Forward / Defender
IRELAND CAPS: 35+
IRELAND GOALS: 1+
DATE OF BIRTH: 26 January, 2000
PLACE OF BIRTH: Ballinasloe (Co. Galway)
CURRENT CLUB: Florida State Seminoles (USA)

PROFILE:

Attack-minded Heather played an important role in Ireland's World Cup qualification, with Vera Pauw often utilising the youngster as the **team's main striker**. For the final World Cup squad, though, Heather was named as a right wing-back – the position she played on her senior debut against Scotland in July 2017, aged 17, and her favoured role. In either position, her **pace and energy** make her a **tricky opponent**. Heather's first international goal came against Iceland in 2021, while she was a student at Florida State University. She featured twice at the World Cup, against Australia and Nigeria.

MARISSA SHEVA

WORLD CUP STAR ★

POSITION: Forward
IRELAND CAPS: 5+
IRELAND GOALS: 0
DATE OF BIRTH: 22 April, 1997
PLACE OF BIRTH: Pennsylvania (USA)
CURRENT CLUB: Washington Spirit (USA)

PROFILE:
Eligible through her Donegal-born grandmother and Tyrone-born grandfather, US-born Marissa was thrilled to make her debut in a green shirt in February 2023 against China PR. Vera Pauw rewarded the **wizard winger** with starts in the next two games against USA. Marissa represented Pennsylvania State University at college in **soccer and athletics**, and is a talented middle-distance runner. She plays her club soccer in **America's top league**, the NWSL, for Washington Spirit. Her next goal is to help her new teammates at Ireland continue to climb the FIFA world rankings.

GREAT GREEN
DENISE O'SULLIVAN

POSITION: Midfielder
IRELAND CAPS: 105+
IRELAND GOALS: 15+
DATE OF BIRTH: 4 February, 1994
PLACE OF BIRTH: Cork (Co. Cork)
CURRENT CLUB: North Carolina Courage (USA)
HEIGHT: 1 m 63 cm
FAVOURED FOOT: Right

PROFILE:
Cork-born Denise O'Sullivan is the **engine at the heart of Ireland's midfield**. Her top technique and playmaking ability have seen her earn over a **century of caps** for the Girls in Green. Not only does she create goals, O'Sullivan is an **important goalscorer** for the national side too. Her first international goals came on her Ireland debut in 2011, where the midfielder scored twice against Wales. Unsurprisingly, she's been one of the **first names on the teamsheet** ever since. At club level, O'Sullivan's football journey has taken her around the world, playing in Ireland, Scotland, Australia, England and the USA's top leagues. **A true superstar!**

FOOTBALL JOURNEY:

One of nine children, Denise's love of football was born on the streets outside her home in Knocknaheeny. She would play for hours each night after school with the boys, while her brother John Paul was capped at junior international level. Her first grassroots team was the boys' club Nufarm Athletic, where she played until the age of 11, at which time mixed-gender football was no longer allowed. While some of the boys were quicker and stronger than she was, **Denise easily matched their skill** on the ball. She then switched to a girls' team – Wilton United – where her talent shone through.

A call-up for Ireland's youth teams followed, with Denise helping her side reach the **final of the 2010 UEFA Under-17 European Championship**, where they lost to Spain in a dramatic penalty shoot-out. That same year, the midfielder scored in the quarter-finals of the FIFA Under-17 World Cup, as Ireland bowed out to Japan. Two outstanding tournaments put the Cork youngster on the radar of some big clubs.

As a teenager, she went on to star for both Cork City and Peamount United, where she was given her **first taste of Champions League football**. But to follow her dream of becoming a professional footballer full-time, Denise knew she had to play abroad.

At the age of 18, Denise agreed a move to Glasgow City, where she quickly became the **club's best player** and starred in the Champions League once again. Here, she had to grow up quickly and put homesickness to the back of her mind to take her game to the next level. In her three seasons in Scotland, **Denise lifted an incredible eight trophies** and in 2014 was part of the first Scottish side to ever reach the quarter-finals of the Champions League.

With each season she played, the young midfielder was becoming stronger and stronger. In 2016, Denise was ready to take the next step on her football journey and test herself in the **toughest league in the world** – the NWSL. A short stint with American side Houston Dash didn't work out, so Denise asked to be traded. When North Carolina Courage came in for her, it turned out to be a **dream move**. Playing as a defensive midfielder, she helped the Courage to win five trophies and was twice voted the club's **Most Valuable Player**.

Loan moves to Australia and England in the off-seasons followed, giving the globe-trotting star the chance to see more of the world than most footballers. To return to Australia with the Girls in Green for the 2023 Women's World Cup was a **special milestone**, as Denise played all three Group games.

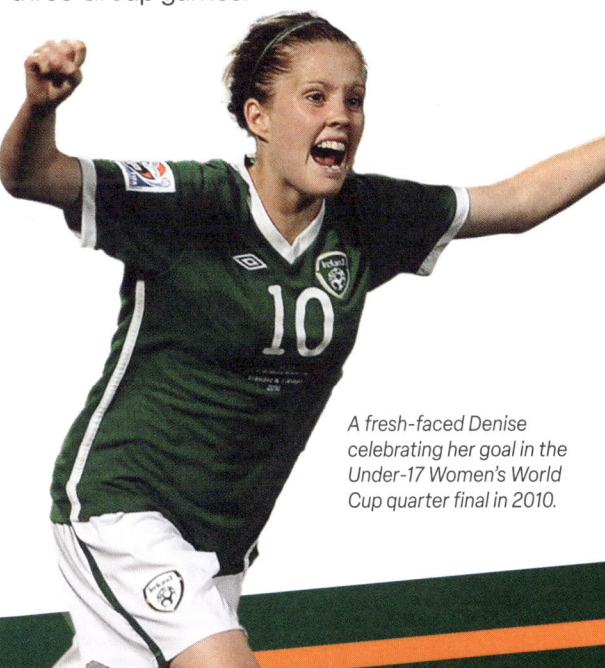

A fresh-faced Denise celebrating her goal in the Under-17 Women's World Cup quarter final in 2010.

THE COACH

VERA PAUW

Born in the Netherlands, Vera won **89 caps for her country** as a player, before **guiding the nation to the semi-finals** of Euro 2009 as head coach. Vera has also coached Scotland, Russia and South Africa, and managed in Thailand. She took the reins as **Ireland's chief coach** in September 2019, and just missed out on qualification for the Women's Euro 2022 in England. Determined to take the Girls in Green to the next level, Vera left no stone unturned in putting together a **talented Irish squad**, made up of players who wear the green shirt with pride. She will go down in history as the first coach to lead Ireland's women to a major tournament.

Vera gives a team talk to her Girls in Green as part of their World Cup preparations.

IRELAND WOMEN'S NATIONAL TEAM HEAD COACHES

- 🇮🇪 Pat NOONE (1973–1974)
- 🇮🇪 Pat NOONE & Dan McGLONE (1974)
- 🇮🇪 Kevin HEALY (1975–1980)
- 🇮🇪 Tony KELLY (1981–1983)
- 🇮🇪 Eamonn DARCY (1984–1985)
- 🇮🇪 Fran ROONEY (1986–1991)
- 🇮🇪 Linda GORMAN (1991–1992)
- 🇮🇪 Mick COOKE (1992–2000)
- 🇮🇪 Noel KING (2000–2010)
- 🇮🇪 Susan RONAN (2010–2016)
- 🏴󠁧󠁢󠁥󠁮󠁧󠁿 Colin BELL (2017–2019)
- 🇳🇱 Vera PAUW (2019–present)

THE FUTURE IS GREEN!

While Ireland's senior side is packed with experienced players, the door is always open to the next generation of talented youngsters whose skills will make the squad even stronger. Here are just a few young players tipped to star for the Girls in Green in the years ahead.

TARA O'HANLON

POSITION: Defender
DATE OF BIRTH: 14 March, 2005
CURRENT CLUB: Peamount United

PROFILE:
Dubliner Tara won her first senior caps in the double header against world champions USA in spring 2023. Still only a teenager, the young Peamount United left-back is predicted to make many more appearances.

KATIE KEANE

POSITION: Goalkeeper
DATE OF BIRTH: 27 July, 2006
CURRENT CLUB: Shelbourne

PROFILE:
The youngest of this fantastic foursome, Dublin-born Katie had a busy year in 2022, featuring for Ireland's Under-16, Under-17 and Under-19 teams as well as being called up to a senior training camp for the first time. With her talent and hard work, she could become Ireland's top stopper one day.

ÉABHA O'MAHONY

POSITION: Defender
DATE OF BIRTH: 17 May, 2002
CURRENT CLUB: Texas Longhorns (USA)

PROFILE:

Éabha has been part of the Irish youth squads since Under-15 level and has previously captained the Under-17s. The biggest match of her career to date was making her senior debut for the Girls in Green in 2019. Her current side is the Longhorns at the University of Texas, where Éabha is studying, having earlier played college soccer at Boston College.

JESSIE STAPLETON

POSITION: Defender
DATE OF BIRTH: 17 May, 2002
CURRENT CLUB: West Ham United (England)

PROFILE:

Jessie grew up playing mixed soccer and joined Shelbourne at 16. Her first senior cap came against Philippines in summer 2022. While she plays in midfield at club level, Vera Pauw believes the teenager's best position may be as a central defender. Jessie joined English WSL club West Ham United ahead of the 2023/24 season.

HALL OF FAME

Over the first five decades of the WNT's history, many talented players have proudly worn the famous green jersey. These women have faced discrimination, poor facilities and coaching, and received little pay or none at all for their tireless efforts. But with each generation, their talent and success has slowly helped the women's game in Ireland to grow. And while there are many more incredible Girls in Green, below are four of the finest players that the Emerald Isle has produced.

LINDA GORMAN

POSITION: Defender
PLAYED FOR IRELAND: 1973–1985
PLACE OF BIRTH: Dublin (Co. Dublin)

Linda Gorman was the left-back and **captain** when Ireland's women played their first official internationals in 1973 – away to Wales and home to Northern Ireland. She is thought to have made more than 25 appearances for the Girls in Green and was the **team's record caps-holder** when she retired in 1985. As well as starring on the pitch, she became **Ireland's first female manager** in 1991, and later became the first female coach to guide a schoolboys' team at Home Farm to a memorable **treble of trophies**. Now in her seventies, Linda plays walking football.

PAULA GORHAM

POSITION: Forward
PLAYED FOR IRELAND: 1973–1978
PLACE OF BIRTH: Dundalk (Co. Louth)

A **pioneer of the women's game in Ireland**, Paula was part of the Dundalk Ladies team who played Corinthians Nomads in a landmark game for women in 1970. Two years later, Paula scored a **hat-trick on her Ireland Women's senior debut** in Wales to win the match 2–3. A tricky centre-forward who could hold up the ball for others and score herself, she went on to make more than 10 appearances in a green jersey. The Football Association of Ireland inducted Paula into their **Hall of Fame** in 2020.

OLIVIA O'TOOLE

POSITION: Forward
PLAYED FOR IRELAND: 1991–2009
PLACE OF BIRTH: Dublin (Co. Dublin)

Only Robbie Keane has scored more goals for Ireland than Olivia, a **fantastic forward** who represented Ireland for almost twenty years. Growing up, Olivia didn't know that an international team for women even existed, but jumped at the chance of a trial, aged 20. She made her debut for the Girls in Green away to Spain in December 1991, in front of 7,000 fans. While Ireland were expected to lose the match, Olivia's solo goal gave the Republic their **first ever win** on continental soil. By the time she retired, the Dublin-born forward had scored an incredible 54 international goals, including a record five hat-tricks. **A class act.**

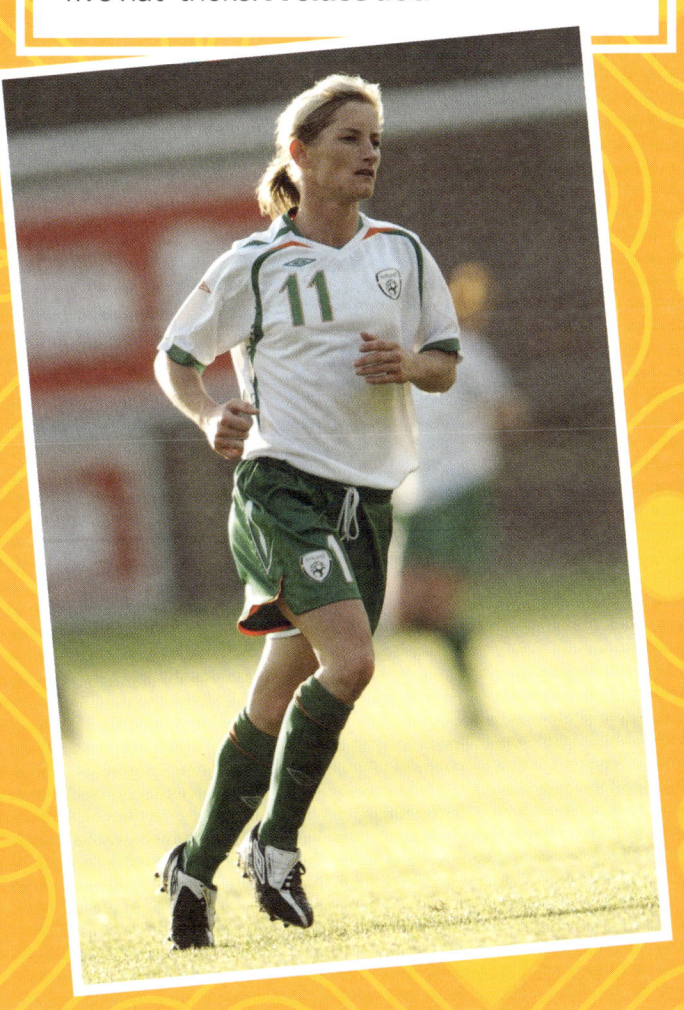

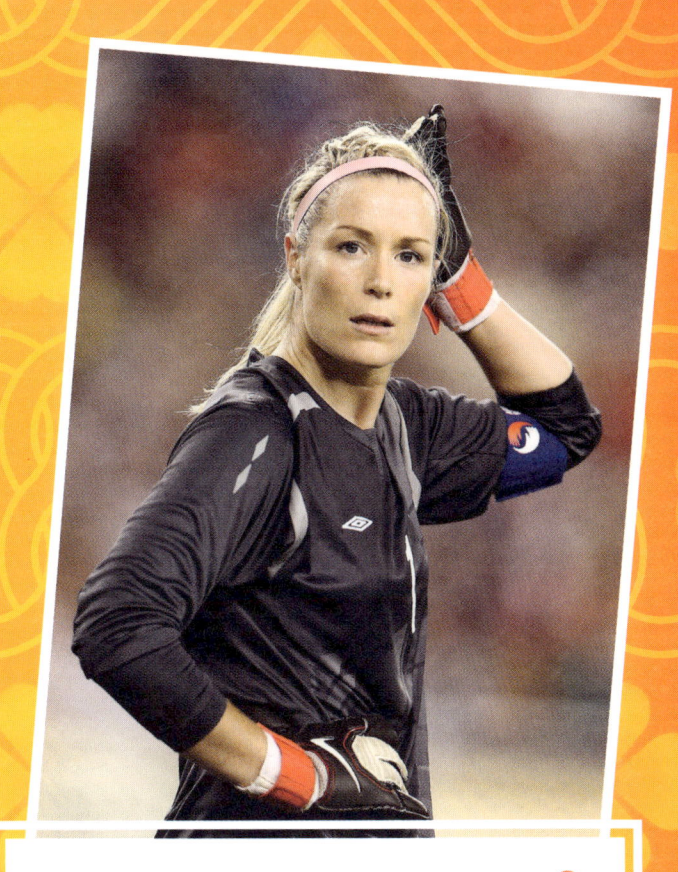

EMMA BYRNE

POSITION: Goalkeeper
PLAYED FOR IRELAND: 1996–2017
PLACE OF BIRTH: Leixlip (Co. Kildare)

An **Irish legend** between the sticks, Emma started playing as a schoolgirl for Leixlip United. It wasn't long before the big clubs came calling and Emma spent a season at Fortuna Hjørring in Denmark, before a move to Arsenal. There, she played a key role in helping the Gunners win 11 league titles and become **European champions** – the only English club to do so. The keeper's international career began as a 16-year-old, who would go on to become the side's record appearance holder, earning 134 caps. A **leader on and off the pitch**, in 2017, Emma led a players' strike that led to better pay and working conditions for the squad, as well as future Girls in Green. Emma was the **first woman** to be inducted into the FAI's Hall of Fame.

GIRLS IN GREEN: DOWN UNDER

In the summer of 2023, Vera Pauw picked a strong squad that combined youth and experience to travel Down Under and make their long-awaited **Women's World Cup debut.** Drawn in a tough group with Australia, Canada and Nigeria, Ireland relished their role as **underdogs** and were determined to make their emerald army of fans proud, whether cheering on the **Girls in Green** in Australia or supporting from back home. Here's how the team's **Australian adventure** unfolded.

GROUP B — AUSTRALIA 1-0 REPUBLIC OF IRELAND

20 July, 2023 — STADIUM AUSTRALIA, SYDNEY

The Girls in Green kicked off their tournament on the opening day of the **ninth edition of the Women's World Cup.** So many fans wanted to watch the match against joint-hosts Australia that it had to be switched to the enormous Stadium Australia in Sydney.

Playing in front of a sell-out crowd of **75,784 fans**, it was the match of their lives for the Girls in Green, who delivered a **battling first-half performance** to keep the score at 0–0 going into the break.

Early in the second half, though, the Matildas earned a penalty. Without their injured star striker Sam Kerr, stand-in skipper Steph Catley converted the spot-kick. **Megan Connolly, Katie McCabe** and **Louise Quinn** all had chances to level the score after that, but the Australian defence stood firm. Despite the defeat, Ireland had **plenty of positives** to take into their next Group B game in Perth.

The starting eleven that took on the Matildas on home soil in Sydney.

60

Ireland's debut goal at a Women's World Cup will be talked about for years to come.

GROUP B — CANADA 2-1 REPUBLIC OF IRELAND

PERTH RECTANGULAR STADIUM, PERTH

26 July, 2023

Captain **Katie McCabe** gave the Girls in Green the **perfect start in Perth** when she scored an 'Olimpico' – a goal direct from a corner – after only four minutes. Ireland's first ever goal at a Women's World Cup was definitely one to remember!

In a **bright first half,** Ireland matched Canada player for player, but a **sucker-punch** came just before half-time, when a Canadian cross swung in and touched Megan Connolly last on its way past Courtney Brosnan into the corner of the Irish net.

The Olympic champions doubled their score early in the second half, when Adriana Leon slotted the ball home to make it 2–1, but Ireland continued to push forward. Chances from **Kyra Carusa** and **more magic from Katie McCabe** followed, but Ireland sadly could not find the equaliser. Despite a **spirited performance,** two defeats in two games in the tournament meant that Ireland could not progress to the knockout stages.

GIRLS IN GREEN: DOWN UNDER

GROUP B — REPUBLIC OF IRELAND 0-0 NIGERIA

31 July, 2023 — **LANG PARK, BRISBANE**

In their third and final Group B game in Brisbane, Ireland were **playing for pride.** The Girls in Green were desperate to reward their incredible travelling support with something to cheer about.

In the first half it was Ireland who enjoyed more possession of the ball and looked the team most likely to break the deadlock. **Katie McCabe** and **Sinead Farrelly** came the closest to scoring in front of more than 24,000 spectators.

The Super Falcons blasted out of the blocks after the break, though, putting Ireland's defence under pressure with a string of attacks. In goal, **Courtney Brosnan** delivered a **Player of the Match performance**, making some stunning saves to keep a clean sheet and frustrating Nigeria's world-class strikers. The match ended goalless, with Ireland claiming a deserved first World Cup point. The Girls in Green were heading home from their debut tournament with a **bright future** ahead of them.

The Girls in Green put in a fine performance to win their first World Cup point.

GROUP B FINAL TABLE

Pos.	Team	Pld	W	D	L	GF	GA	GD	Pts
1	Australia	3	2	0	1	7	3	4	6
2	Nigeria	3	1	2	0	3	2	1	5
3	Canada	3	1	1	1	2	5	-3	4
4	**Rep. Ireland**	**3**	**0**	**1**	**2**	**1**	**3**	**-2**	**1**

WOMEN'S WORLD CUP 2023 SQUAD

#	Player	Apps.	Goals
1	COURTNEY **BROSNAN**	3	0
2	CLAIRE **O'RIORDAN**	0	0
3	CHLOE **MUSTAKI**	0	0
4	LOUISE **QUINN**	3	0
5	NIAMH **FAHEY**	3	0
6	MEGAN **CONNOLLY**	3	0
7	DIANE **CALDWELL**	(1)	0
8	RUESHA **LITTLEJOHN**	3	0
9	AMBER **BARRETT**	(2)	0
10	DENISE **O'SULLIVAN**	3	0
11	KATIE **McCABE** (C)	3	1
12	LILY **AGG**	1 (1)	0
13	ÁINE **O'GORMAN**	1	0
14	HEATHER **PAYNE**	2	0
15	LUCY **QUINN**	1 (1)	0
16	GRACE **MOLONEY**	0	0
17	SINEAD **FARRELLY**	3	0
18	KYRA **CARUSA**	3	0
19	ABBIE **LARKIN**	(3)	0
20	MARISSA **SHEVA**	1 (2)	0
21	CIARA **GRANT**	0	0
22	IZZY **ATKINSON**	(3)	0
23	MEGAN **WALSH**	0	0

Substitute appearances are shown in brackets.

Thousands of fans gathered in O'Connell Street to welcome back their World Cup heroes.

NEXT STEPS

Not content with appearing at one major tournament, the **Girls in Green will go again** on a journey to try to qualify for the Women's Euro 2025, set to be hosted by Switzerland. This time, the squad and coaches hope to build on their progress made in Australia and New Zealand and take on the **best teams in Europe**.

The Girls in Green can't wait to pull on the Ireland shirt again after their incredible World Cup journey.

The very **first Women's Nations League** begins in September 2023, with the finals in February 2024. This **new competition** will reveal which teams will represent Europe at the 2024 Paris Summer Olympics and decide how teams will line up for the European Qualifying phase for the Women's Euro 2025.

Denise O'Sullivan will be looking to add to her goal tally in the Nations League fixtures.

64

COMING SOON!

The Girls in Green feature in League B of the Nations League and have been drawn against Northern Ireland, Hungary and Albania. As the **highest-ranked nation** in the group, Ireland will be aiming to top their group to put them in a strong position for the European Qualifiers phase for the **Women's Euro 2025**.

The Aviva Stadium will host the Girls in Green's home fixture against Northern Ireland – the team's first-ever match at the national stadium.

NORTHERN IRELAND
FIFA WORLD RANKING: 45

Two sides that know each other's game well, the WNT have unsurprisingly played neighbours Northern Ireland more than any other nation. With some **experienced players** including Simone Magill and top scorer Rachel Furness in their ranks, Ireland will not underestimate their opponents from across the border. The Girls in Green ran out **4–0 winners** the last time the sides met, back in 2018.

23 September, 2023	Rep. Ireland v Northern Ireland
5 December, 2023	Northern Ireland v Rep. Ireland

ALBANIA
FIFA WORLD RANKING: 72

A team that only formed in 2011, the Girls in Green will meet Albania for the **first time** at senior level. While Ireland are expected to win all six points against their **lower-ranked opponents**, they will be careful not to slip up against the Red and Blacks. The away fixture will be played at the National Arena in Albania's capital Tirana, while Tallaght is the likely home venue. Albania's most-capped player is midfielder Luçije Gjini, while forward Megi Doçi is their leading scorer.

27 October, 2023	Rep. Ireland v Albania
31 October, 2023	Albania v Rep. Ireland

HUNGARY
FIFA WORLD RANKING: 41

The Girls in Green have faced Hungary on **seven previous occasions**, with their most recent meeting played at the Cyprus Cup in 2017, which ended in a stalemate. The **highest-ranked of Ireland's three opponents**, their squad mainly play their club football at home in Hungary, while a handful of players star in the women's Bundesliga in Germany and the Italian women's Serie A. Hungary are yet to qualify for a major tournament.

26 September, 2023	Hungary v Rep. Ireland
1 December, 2023	Rep. Ireland v Hungary

GO FOR GLORY!

You've read all about the superstars that make up the squad, now test your knowledge of the Girls in Green in the quiz below. Will you score a perfect 10?

1. WHICH GROUND DOES THE TEAM CALL 'HOME'?

- [ ] A. Richmond Park
- [✓] B. Aviva Stadium
- [ ] C. Tallaght Stadium

2. WHICH NATION DID IRELAND BEAT IN THE WORLD CUP PLAY-OFF MATCH TO QUALIFY FOR THE TOURNAMENT?

- [ ] A. Northern Ireland
- [ ] B. England
- [✓] C. Scotland

3. WHO IS THE RECORD CAPS HOLDER FOR THE IRELAND WOMEN'S NATIONAL TEAM?

- [✓] A. Louise Quinn
- [ ] B. Áine O'Gorman
- [ ] C. Emma Byrne

4. HOW OLD WAS KATIE MCCABE WHEN SHE FIRST CAPTAINED THE GIRLS IN GREEN?

- [ ] A. 18
- [✓] B. 21
- [ ] C. 24

5. HOW MANY POINTS DID IRELAND WIN AT THE 2023 WOMEN'S WORLD CUP IN AUSTRALIA AND NEW ZEALAND?

- [✓] A. Zero
- [ ] B. One
- [ ] C. Two

6. WHAT IS THE NATIONALITY OF IRELAND'S WORLD CUP COACH, VERA PAUW?

- [ ] A. Polish
- [✓] B. Dutch
- [ ] C. American

7. WHO DID IRELAND BEAT IN THEIR RECORD 11-0 VICTORY?

- [ ] A. Slovakia
- [✓] B. Georgia
- [ ] C. Finland

8. HOW MANY PLAYERS IN THE CURRENT GIRLS IN GREEN SQUAD HAVE WON MORE THAN 100 CAPS?

- [ ] A. Three
- [✓] B. Four
- [ ] C. Five

Look back through the book if you're stuck!

9. IN WHICH COUNTRY WAS GOALKEEPER COURTNEY BROSNAN BORN?

- [ ] A. Ireland
- [ ] B. England
- [✓] C. United States

10. WHAT COLOUR IS THE TEAM'S AWAY SHIRT?

- [ ] A. Orange
- [✓] B. White
- [ ] C. Green

The answers are on page 69.

GROWING THE GAME

If reading this book has inspired you to get **closer to the action**, there has never been a better time to get involved – whether as a fan, a player or a grassroots volunteer. So whether you're new to the game or finding your feet again, look out for a local club where a **warm welcome awaits**.

#COYGIG

#OUTBELIEVE

ANSWERS

GO FOR GLORY!

1. C. Tallaght Stadium
2. C. Scotland
3. C. Emma Byrne
4. B. 21
5. B. One
6. B. Dutch
7. B. Georgia
8. B. Four
9. C. United States
10. B. White

PHOTO CREDITS

The publishers would like to thank the following sources for their kind permission to reproduce the pictures in this book.

Cover:

All © Stephen McCarthy / Sportsfile

Interiors:

Alamy: PA Images / Alamy Stock Photo: 6t, 16–17, 66tl

Getty Images: Seb Daly / Sportsfile 10br, 17, 33, 58r, 68t; Laurence Griffiths / FIFA 53; Icon Sportswire 7br, 28, 50, 52; Stephen McCarthy / Sportsfile 5l, 5c, 5r, 6tl, 6–7b, 7tl, 7tc, 7bc, 8–9, 11br, 12–13, 13, 14t, 14b, 19, 20, 21, 23, 24, 30, 31, 36, 37, 38, 39, 41, 42, 43, 44, 45, 46, 49, 51, 54–55, 54b, 56l, 57t, 57b, 61, 62, 63, 64–65, 64b, 66bc, 66br2, 67tr, 68b; Ben McShane / Sportsfile 6c, 56r; Stephanie Meek / CameraSport 47; Brendan Moran / Sportsfile 6bl, 7tr, 7cl, 27, 29, 34, 35, 40, 48; Mick O'Shea 25; Christian Petersen 11cl, 18l, 59r, 66br1; Brad Smith / USSF 32–33, 66bl; Brendan Thorne 60; John Todd / USSF 26; Omar Vega 22, 67bl

National Football Museum (United Kingdom): 6–7c, 10–11t

Sportsfile: Stephen McCarthy 11tl, 58l; Brendan Moran 11tr, 18r, 59l

Every effort has been made to acknowledge correctly and contact the source and/or copyright holder of each picture. Any unintentional errors or omissions will be corrected in future editions of this book.